TAEKWONDO
COLORING BOOK

PAINTO LAB

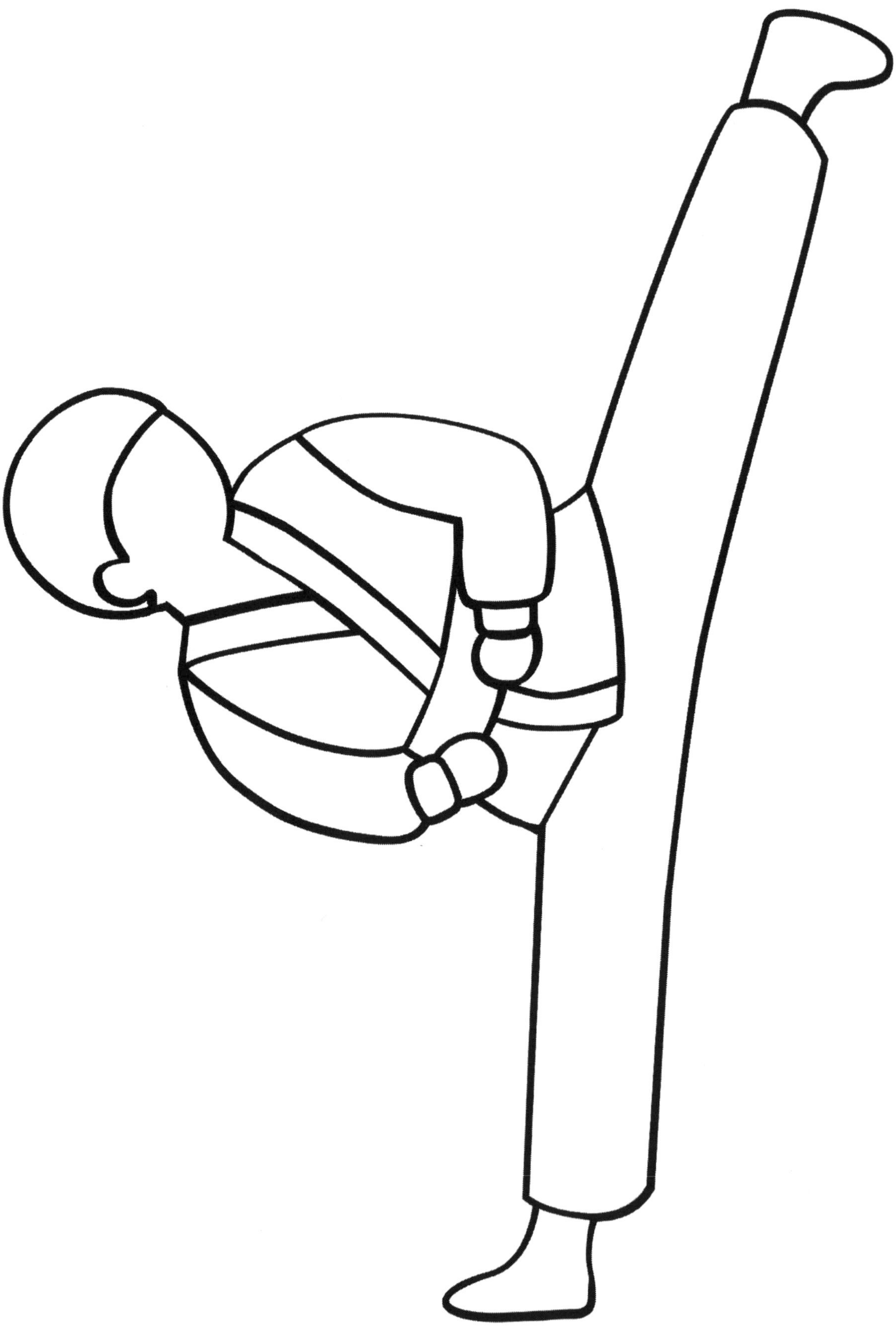

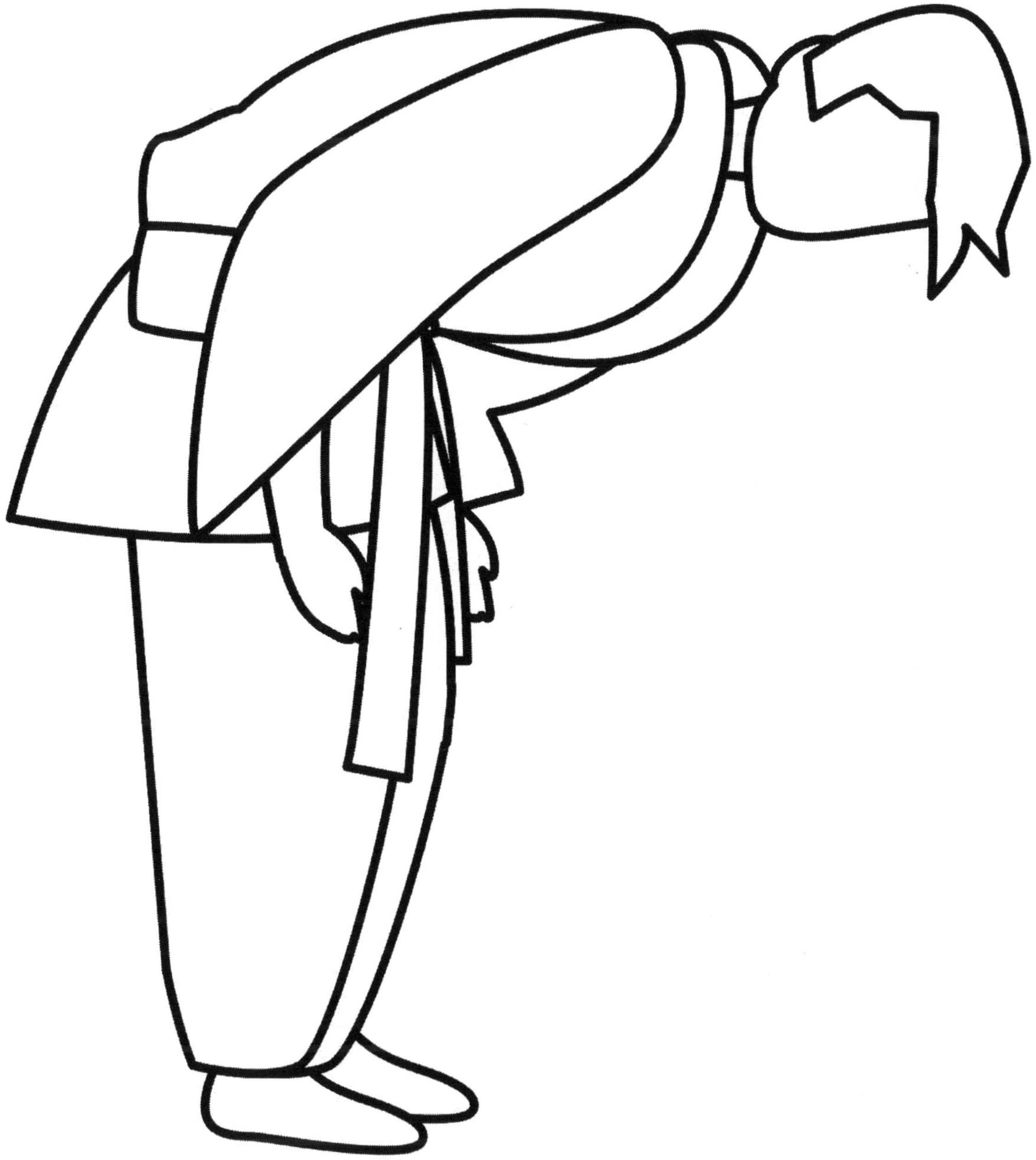

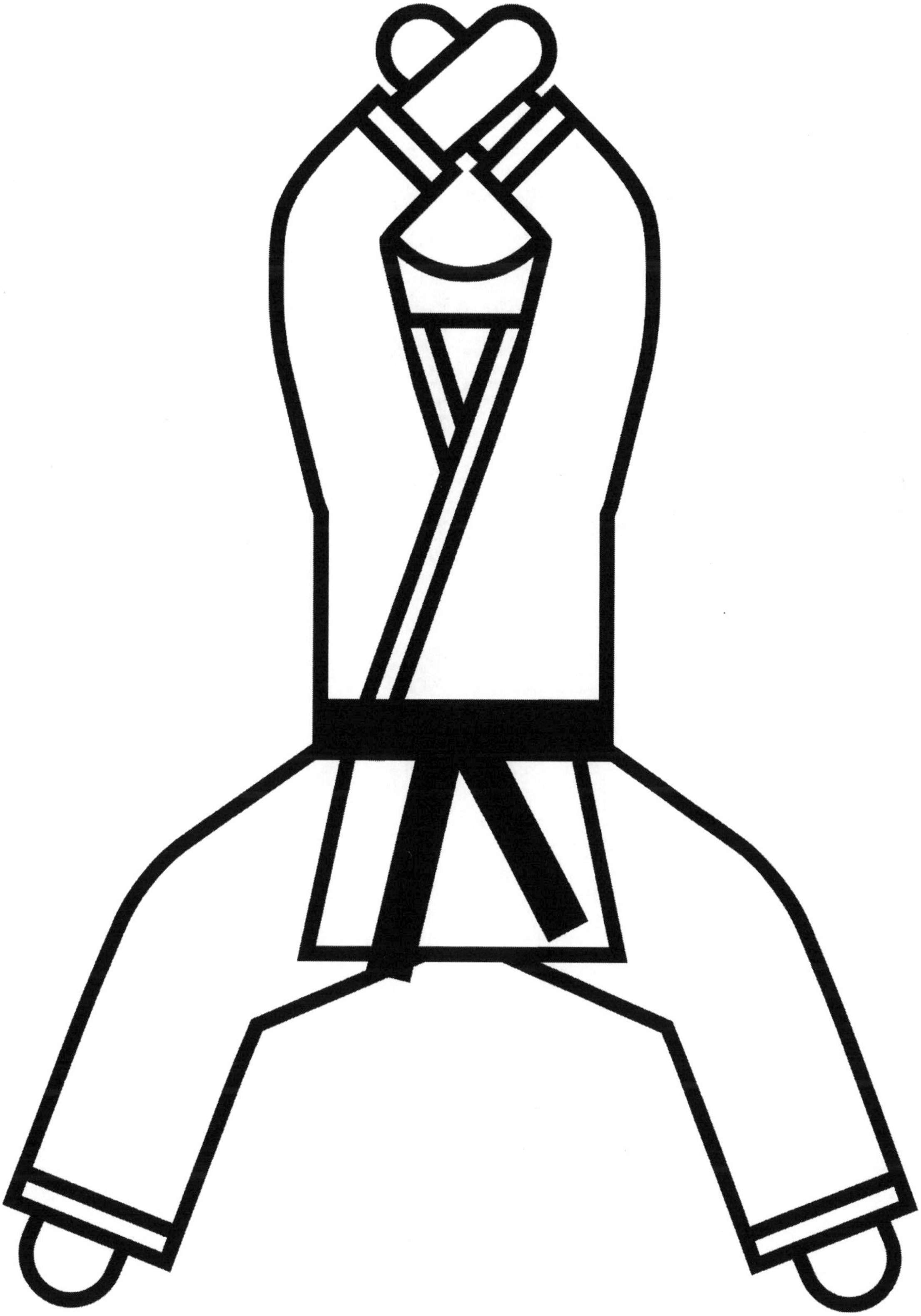

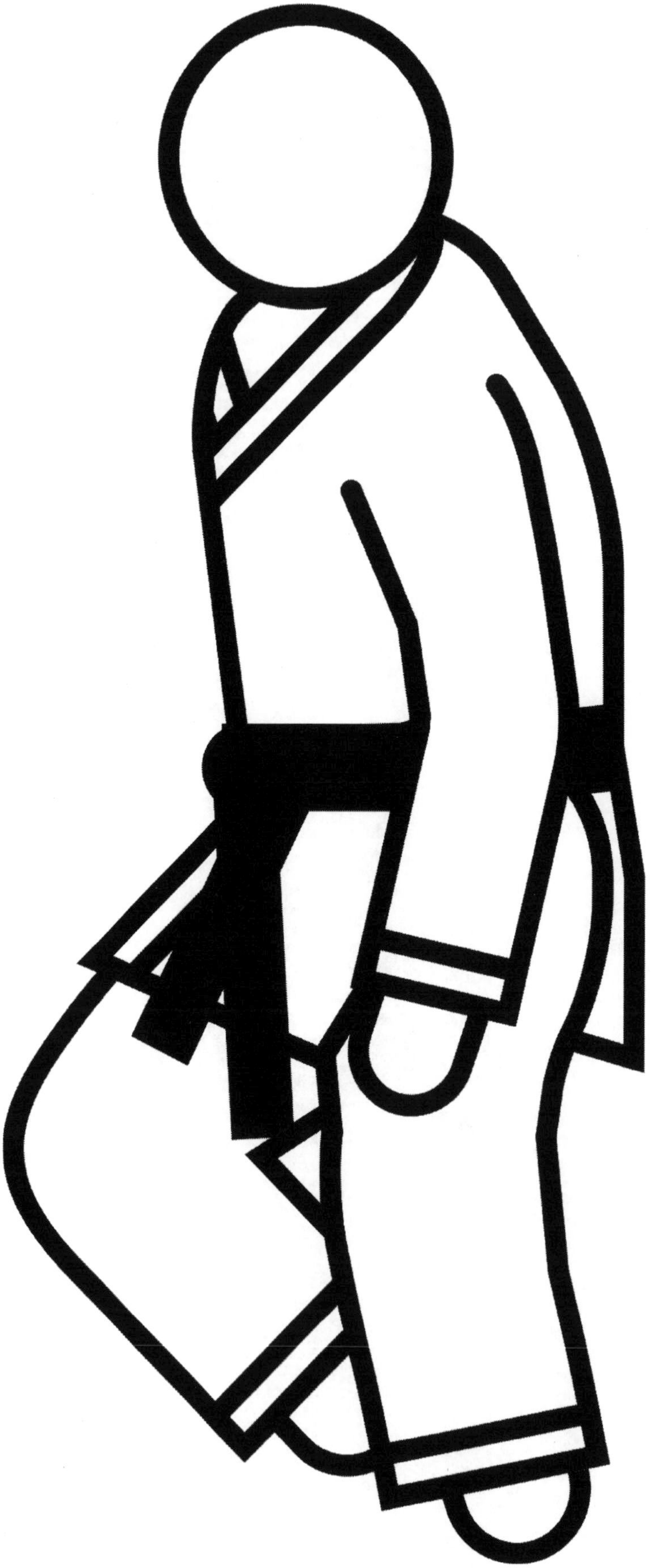

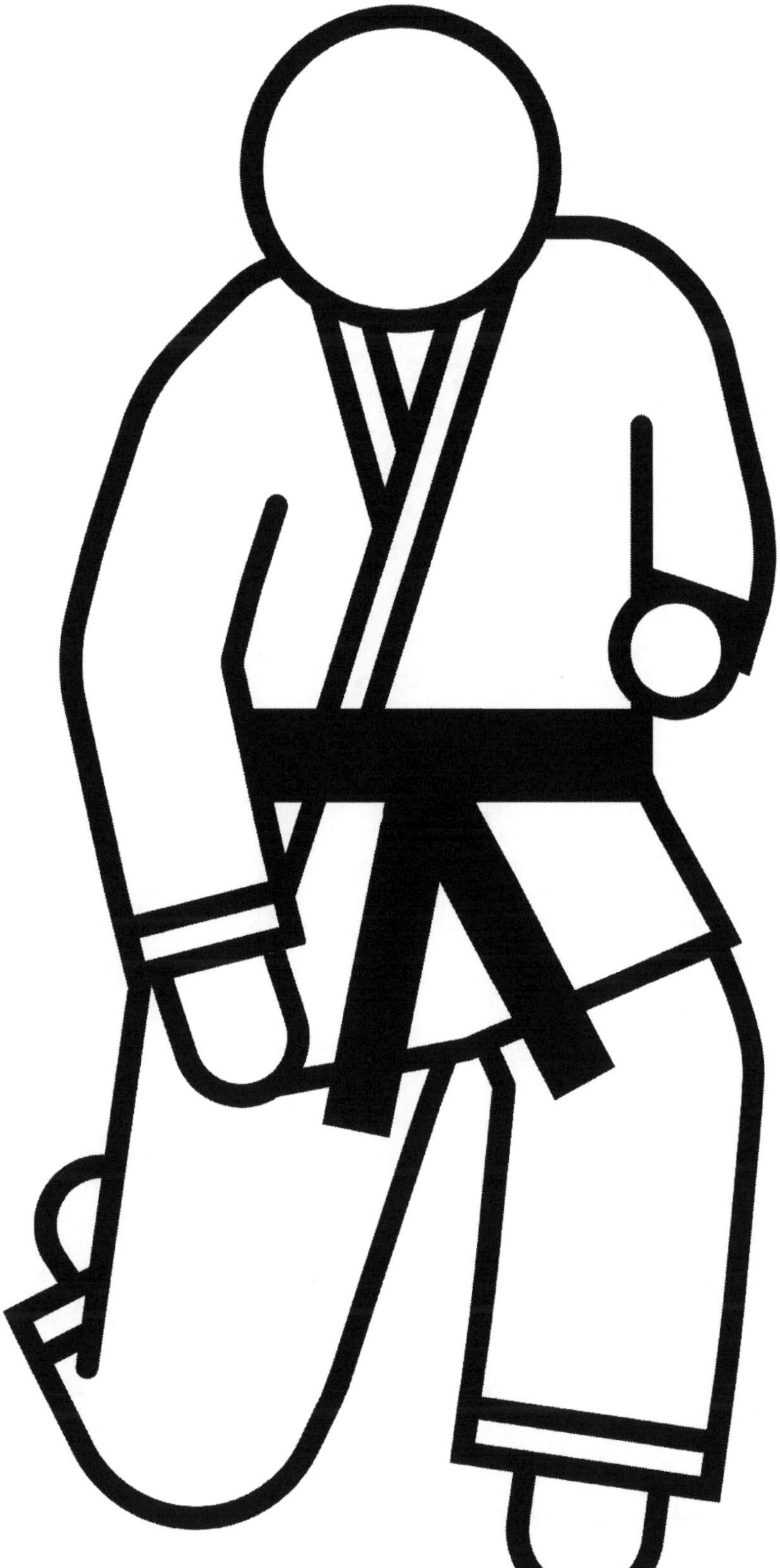

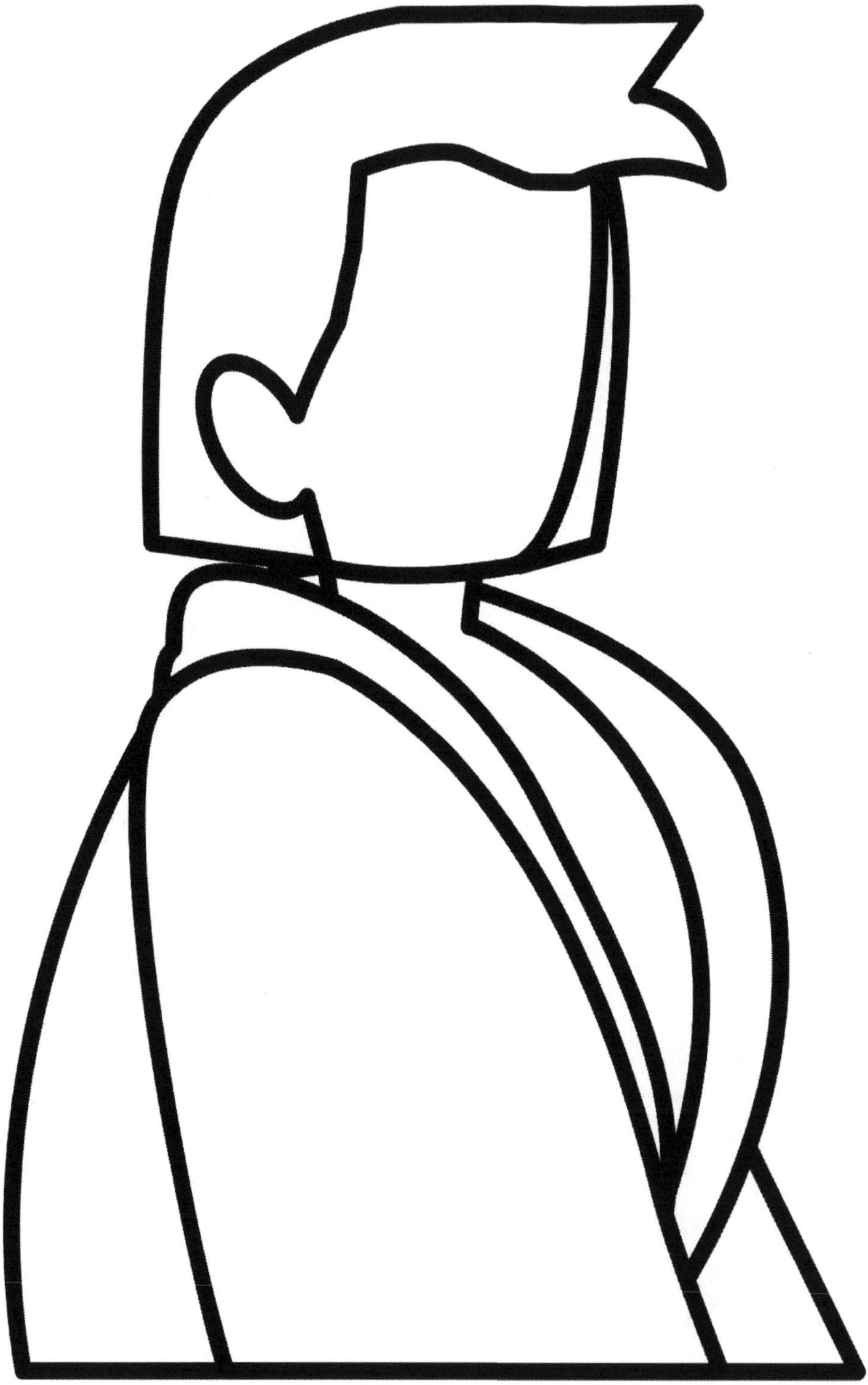

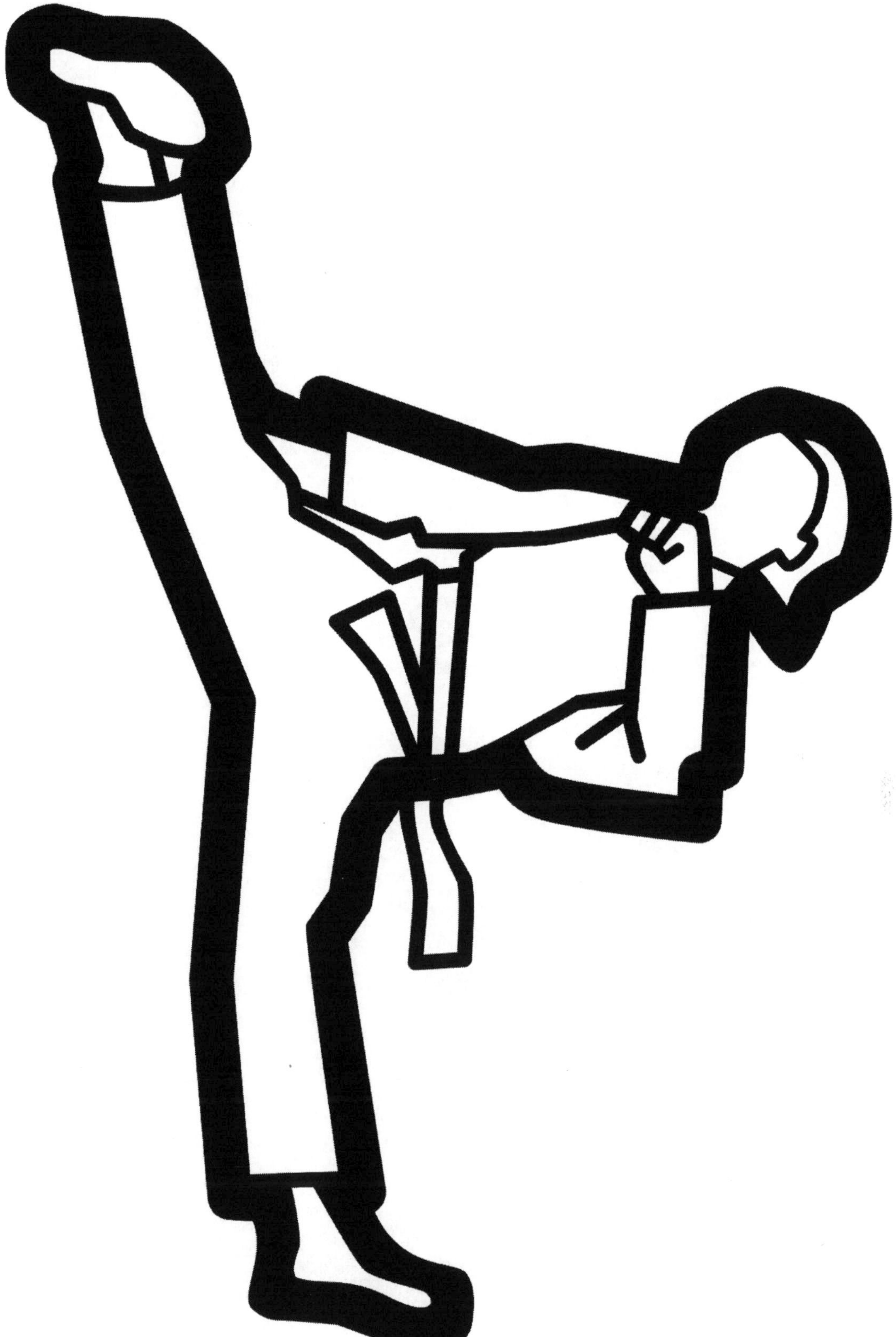

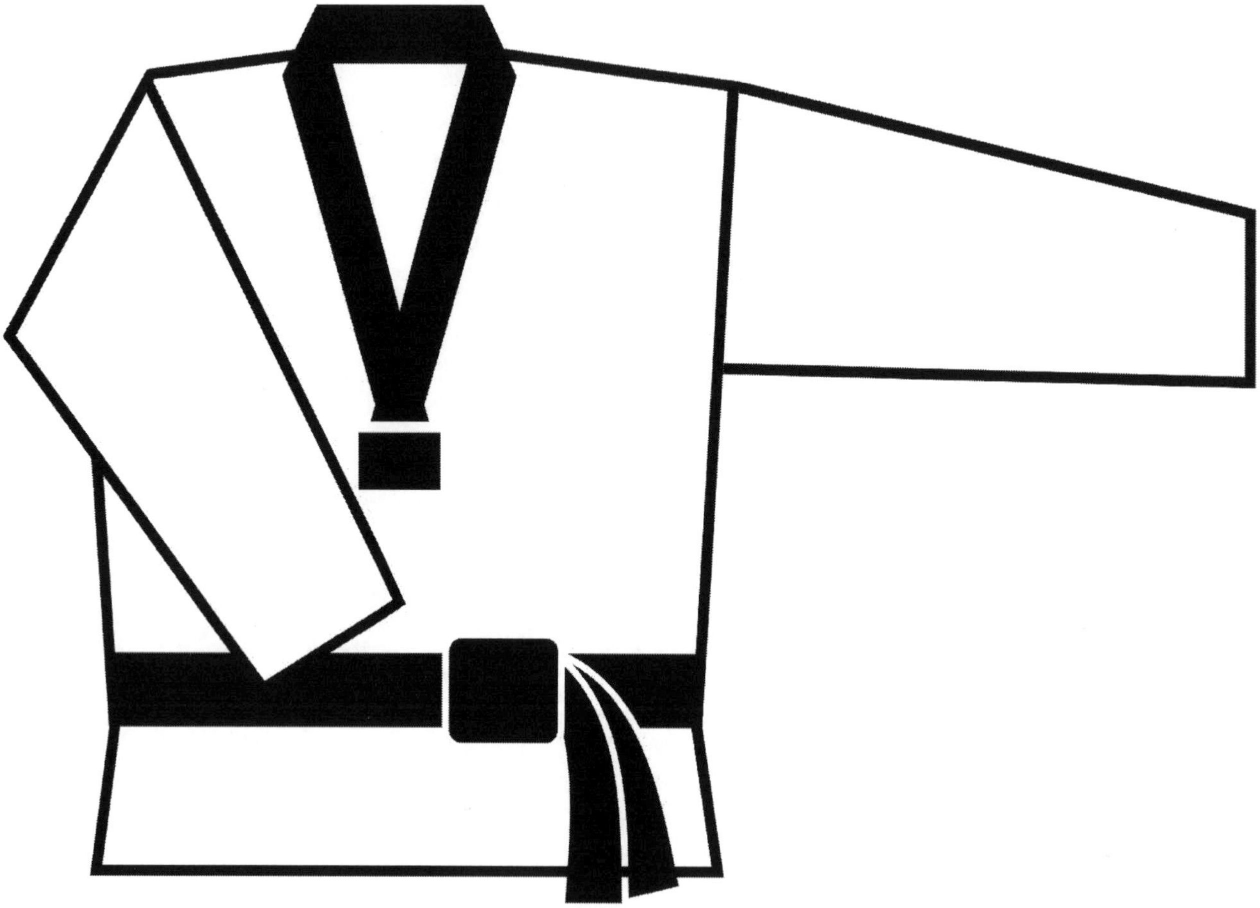

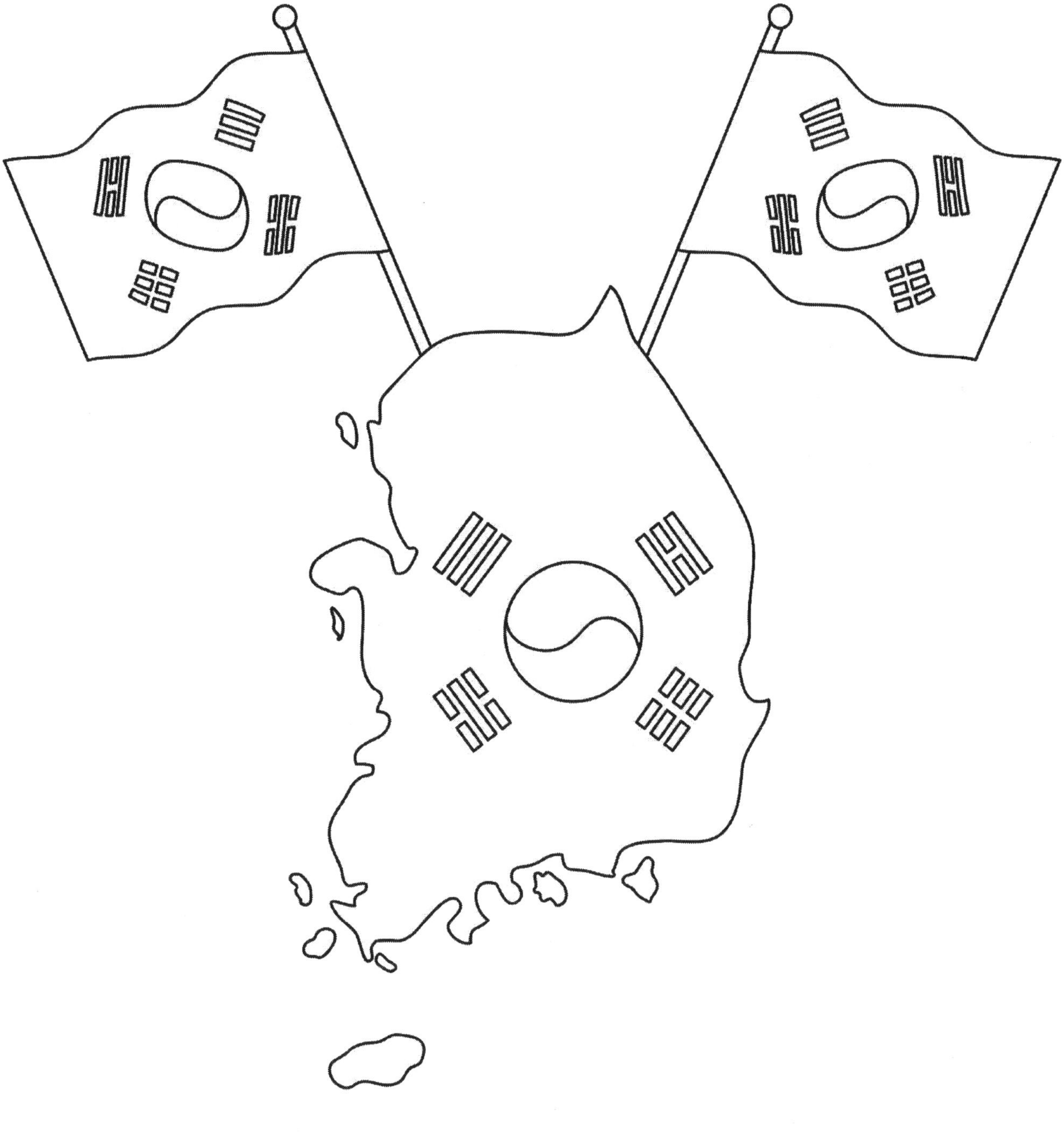

Made in the USA
Middletown, DE
17 March 2023

26864151R00018

ISBN 9798550381076
9 798550 381076
900